Words While We Walk Together

A Collection by and for
Tonia Teresa Healey

RoseDog Books
PITTSBURGH, PENNSYLVANIA 15238

RoseDog Books
585 Alpha Drive
Suite 103
Pittsburgh, PA 15238

Visit our website at *www.rosedogbookstore.com*

ISBN: 979-8-89127-547-8
eISBN: 979-8-89127-045-9

Words While We Walk Together

Introduction

There is nothing better than a good walk!

A walk can clear the mind and invigorate the body. It can get us to where we are going or leave a nuisance behind. It can follow the straight and narrow or meander the crooked path. More often than not, we walk in circles. Ending up right back where we started.

From our first steps to our last, walking is a wonderful metaphor for the journey of our living. We mark time and space by how we navigate through it. Our walk is sometimes a crawl, or a run, perhaps even a dance.

Better still, is when we do those things together — when we walk together.

Words While We Walk Together is a collection of work by and for Tonia. It marks the intersection of paths through the years, of experiences along the way, and of people and places of importance.

Walking Toward the Light

Walking in Search of Possibilities

Walking in the Darkness

Walking with a Love

Walking at the Water's Edge

Walking with a Friend

Walking with My Family

Walking Toward an End

Table of Contents

All of the works in the book were composed by Tonia T. Healey except where authorship by friends and family is noted.

Walking

Toward the Light

Getting to Brown – Trauma and Resolution

Getting to Brown was a story in itself! I was already 35 years old, had 2 boys, was divorced from my husband Jack, had worked as a nurse in various settings, including Mass General Hospital ICU and finally moving back to RI. I was working at the Mental Health Retardation Hospitals, State Institution For Mental Health, sometimes-double shifts to pay the mortgage & support my children. Jack had become an alcoholic having not passed the final step in the Foreign Medical School exam so he could practice medicine in this country. I bought a house in Warwick RI to be closer to both families for support, and went to work at the MHRH. I was pregnant with David at that time. After about three years, still working at the MHRH the union there went on strike and there were picket lines and angry protestors but the nurses went to work. As I was going into the institutional grounds, workers were blocking the roads yelling and hitting my car with sticks, I panicked and pushed down on what I thought was the brake pedal, but it was the gas pedal! Propelling my car into the crowd. I went through the crowd and pulled over to the side of the road, only then did I know that I had hit someone! The police and rescue came and I was taken to the station.

I was tried in Superior Court charges were, Involuntary Vehicular Manslaughter and since I didn't know the outcome of the trial, I had to prepare for the boys for an indefinite time in someone else's care. This was the most difficult thing I had ever done. Neither of the related families could accept the responsibility for them so with the assistance of a friend and Doctor who had delivered both boys we found a great home for them with his friends.

When it was over, I stood before a judge who said, "I have to have you serve time to send a message to the unions and to you that this behavior will not be tolerated". My sentence was thirty days in the Women's Prison in RI and three years with a driver's license suspension. So there I was, a pretty bad mess, no job, no driving, two boys age's three and nine in temporary foster care, and a single mom who had fallen into a very deep hole. How did I get there? Where could I go from here?

To answer that question I have to replay the past journeying back to the beginning that I can remember. The most significant memory is that during all those years I do not remember ever making one decision on my own. You have to understand that this was the 1950' s-1960 and my father was a high-ranking Doctor in the US Army who had friends like General Patton and General MacArthur. So you can see why my parents were strict and had a view of what was proper for a young girl. This even included college and nursing schools. Since medical parents surrounded me, it was given that both my sisters and I would be professional nurses.

After High School in Stuttgart Germany I was sent to live with my Aunt in Rhode Island and attend salve Regina College in the Nursing Program (my sister Donna was already enrolled there) I didn't have any say in where I would attend college it was already done for me by my parents. I did poorly at college in part because I could not adjust to being "on my own" partly because I was not used to the strict "catholic" way of life presented by the college. My parents and younger brother & sister returned from Germany and were assigned to Fort Hood Texas. One year later they were transferred to Fort Meade in Maryland. I was not doing well in college so my parents decided to bring me down to Washington and put me in a hospital nursing school. I was entered into Washington Hospital Center School of Nursing and so was my older sister. There was another move to a different state and a different nursing school. Emotionally I enjoyed the hospital setting more than the collage setting so I was less depressed and more involved with life. That lasted about another year when my father retired from the army and took a job in RI with the state department of health. He was appointed to head the Mental Health Retardation and Hospitals in Cranston, RI and would live on the grounds. I was then enrolled at The Pawtucket Hospital School of Nursing.

From birth my parents made all decisions regarding everything in my life from where we would travel, to what schools I would attend, to my friends and even my 'boyfriends' (in high school it was frowned upon to date an enlisted soldiers son, it must be an officers son) so I dated and fell in love for the first time with Griff Jones who's Father was an officer, and that was my choice entirely, probably the first decision I ever made on my own. And strangely enough Griff & I are still in touch with one another. Later in senior year I did date and fall in love with Ralph who was not an officers son. I loved having someone close that I could share affection with.

When it came to being married, the pressure was high, after dating Jack for five years, my father said "either you get married or I am going to send you to Europe".

We had a lovely wedding in the chapel at Quonset Point, RI. We looked like the perfect couple, both fathers were Doctors, Mom was a nurse as was I, Jacks' brothers were physicians as was he, so it looked like we would live and prosper! But to borrow Morgan's words, Boy was I wrong!!

The first awakening was in reality, "The Honeymoon" oh yes it was really fun, but maybe too much fun! Jack drank endlessly and never got out of bed until noon, of course I was right behind.

I really didn't know who I was as I had made it this far in life being whoever you wanted me to be at the time. I could slip easily from the knowledgeable caring nurse, to the abused wife, to the loving mother, to the party girl, to the gardener who grew and canned all her own vegetables, multiple persons helped manage the chaos of my life. The funny thing was, I didn't see it as chaos. I just went on and on, I had friends, I had family, I had a good job wherever I went, and I denied the behavior of my abusive alcoholic husband.

When I first met Jack he was an intern at Memorial Hospital in Pawtucket RI where I was a nursing student. My parents lived at the state institutions at Howard where my father was director of MHRH and I lived at school or at home with my family. I never questioned Jacks education, as I believed he was a graduate of the University of Paris, Medical school and he was here doing an internship. I didn't know the process for foreign medical doctors to practice in the United States so I never asked about his education. I believed that he was doing an "internship"; he did tell me that he had an exam to pass for his license. In 1963 I graduated from nursing school but continued to work there and lived with my parents. Jack and I continued our relationship for the next few years, until we married in 1965. All this time I was not aware that Jack had not completed the graduation requirements for medical school and also that he was allowed to 'practice medicine' in a hospital as an intern or resident for the total of five years in RI.

Our first home was at the Dr. Joseph H Ladd School in Exeter, RI where Jack had secured a position as a "house physician" mostly due to my father who had some influence in the state. I also worked at the school while pregnant with Joe. After Joe was born I pressured Jack to return to Paris and officially graduate from Medical school, which he did. Joe & I went to Paris when he was 9 months old and lived there for a few months while Jack was completing his graduation requirements. We lived at Ladd School until Jack could no longer practice medicine in RI. Although he had completed the requirements for medical school, he still had not passed the foreign medical school exam (ECFMG)

By 1968 we had moved to Boston because Jack had used up all the years he was allowed to practice in RI without a license, and a friend secured a position at Somerville Hospital in the Emergency department. The law allowed him to practice in Massachusetts for five years. Joe was then two years old. I secured a position at MGH in the ICU, second shift and Jack worked days then took care of Joe in the evening. The next three years went from bad to worse as Jack continued to drink heavily and became very physically abusive to me. After awhile, I couldn't take it anymore and reached out to the Healey brothers and my family for help. They all encouraged me to move back to RI to be closer to the family so in late 1971 I purchased a house in Warwick with money I had saved and bonds left from our wedding gifts. When we moved, I had no idea that I was already pregnant with David, which came as a welcome as I had lost a baby boy two years before.

The move was a good decision and although Jack couldn't work, he continued to take the exam and we had family support near at hand. I went to work at the Institute of Mental Health on the day shift with lots of overtime; Joe was enrolled at St. Timothy's school. We settled into Warwick, had great neighbors who became good friends and while pregnant with David I built a huge garden in the back yard and grew every vegetable you could want. Jack went to various workshops to study for the exam, but what I didn't know at the time was that he also continued to drink heavily while away. David was born in May of 1972 at Memorial Hospital, delivered by Dr. Byron Quinn. Jack was going to stay home and care for him while I worked.

Did I ever give a thought as to what would happen in the future? No, I did not. Remember this was the 70's. Women hardly had rights or voices, so I just went along from day-to-day making the best home for my family as I could and tolerating the abuse and neglect. I was "the good nurse", the "good mother" and the tolerant wife. But everything came crashing down one sunny day in Warwick!

My job at IMH allowed me to run home at 'lunch break' when necessary so one day I did that and as I entered the door to the house I heard David crying very loudly, going in the door I was horrified at what I saw! Jack was passed out on the sofa, drunk and David was in his infant carrier in front of the TV screaming and soaking wet!! And so began my real nightmare!!

I had had it! But what to do now? I had no idea of where to begin to care for my family and to keep all of us safe. I called upon both families for help; Jack's brothers got him admitted to an alcohol detox/rehab hospital, to give me time to pull myself together. After Jack left the hospital he went to live with his brother Stephen who was separated from Connie at the time living in the same neighborhood in Providence. They both were alcoholics so obviously it was a housing situation nightmare for everyone. By this time I had consulted a lawyer (Vincent Cianci) who I had known for years and he advised a separation and restraining order. When Jack became aware of this action he became so angry that he came to the house and broke down the front storm door trying to get to me. For the next few months I continued to work and had a baby sitter in home for David, and Jack had visitation. I filed for divorce in early 1973. This was extremely difficult, being catholic and having a strong catholic family on both sides, it was not looked on as the thing one should do, but given the circumstances I had to protect the boys and myself. The very sad part was that I had never stopped loving Jack; the other sad part was that I had no idea of how to behave or what I should do. The divorce was fmal in March of 1974, Jack was living somewhere in Pawtucket still drinking although he did visit the boys sober, I continued to work at the IMH and had support from the staff, friends in the neighborhood and family. To say that I was not depressed would be a lie, but I had no idea that I was, even though I was working in Mental Health, denial was very strong. I did date and party a bit when friends were available. Depression had been a constant companion for me off an on ever since I had stopped living at home, through one year at Salve Regina College, one year at Washington Hospital Center then another two years at Memorial Hospital in RI. The depression was masked by work and my desire to become a nurse although my behavior during those years was at times irresponsible.

So life went on in Warwick, Joe was in school at St. Timothy's and David home with a babysitter during the day when I worked at the IMH day shift. My divorce from Jack was in progress and he was living in various places but still drinking, he did see the boys but was very angry with me because divorce was not condoned in the Catholic Church. It was difficult to live like this with barely enough money to pay the bills and care for the boys but both of the families were supportive although did not favor a divorce due to religious reasons. You have to understand that this was the 1970's and both families were strong Catholics, they understood the problem and supported caring for Jack with the hope that he would stop drinking and we would be back together. This was not going to happen. Jack had entirely given up on taking the exam so medicine was out and so was his life. It was really sad to see such a warm and talented man with a true gift for surgery spiral down to what he had become. And with my grief, came more depression, which I ignored and continued on with my hectic life.

I began dating first, one of the attendants at the IMH and then a Doctor. My divorce was fmal in March of 1974, although it really didn't matter to me because it changed nothing. Then everything changed in a flash!

It was the early Spring of 1975 the staff of the IMH (caregivers, housekeepers, maintenance,) were unionized and decided to strike at the State Institution for higher wages. The professional Staff was not going to join them but rallied in support. It was a crazy time in my life and I was also drinking to suppress the ongoing depression. I truly did not know how the alcohol inhibited common sense and so the depression bloomed into suicidality. I had been that depressed before having been hospitalized a few times for suicidal intent and attempts. You would think that a single mom with children at home would not venture into that dark space but I did; that dark person inside could not go away for any reason because it had been there for such a long time. I think it was actually because my mind was able to switch from one person to another, where the highs were one person and the lows were another.

On that fate full day I had been out, with whom I don't remember or where, but I came home late and let the babysitter go home, the boys were asleep so I sat at the kitchen table and had another drink or two. I don't remember what happened next except that I obviously was profoundly depressed, tearful and attempted to cut myself, for attention or treatment or because I truly wanted it all to stop. As it became morning I realized that I should be going to work, ignoring that I had had little sleep, too much to drink the night before and was severely depressed but there was my friend the Doctor that I was dating at the time and he lived there at the IMH, so I felt that I should go and see him before going to work. I got in the car and drove off.

As I approached the Medical Center through the back entrance via Pontiac Ave., there were protesters lining the street and the entrance to the IMH with banners and bats and they were very angry having been there most of the night. Most of the workers knew me and knew my car but that didn't stop them from yelling for me to stop and not enter the grounds, as I pulled forward I attempted to tell them I was not going to the Hospital but to see my friend the Doctor, but they wouldn't hear me. They were barricading the street and I pulled up to the line of people, they began yelling and banging on my car doors, windows, hood and roof. I was terrified! My car continued to roll towards them, I had to stop, I put my foot on the brake... But it was THE GAS PEDAL!! My car lunged forward right into the mob of people; I heard screams and yelling then came to a stop a few feet from the line of people that had blocked the road. I pulled over the curb and covered my head in my hands but did not move from the car. The Police arrived quickly, opened the car door and asked me to go with them. When we arrived at the station a few minutes away I was asked for my identification and led to a room where another officer came in and asked me if I knew what happened. I told him what I knew and then...

The police officer told me that I had run over and killed a person who had been in front of my car standing in the road.

They then arrested me and charged me with involuntary vehicular manslaughter. After spending the day there I was taken home by the police officer. My parents had been called earlier to go to my home and care for the boys so they were all there when I arrived in what I can only now imagine was the worst mess of my life.

It was time for me to make decisions on my own! I needed to be honest with myself and the people I loved. One of my cousins referred me to a great lawyer, Eugene F Toro. I would tell the court that I was responsible and I would take responsibility for my actions. And so as I said above I stood before a judge in Providence Superior Court and received my punishment. I was for thirty days in prison with three years of a suspended drivers license. Yes, it could have been much worse.

Thankfully it was not longer. I was given a few days to get my life in order but I had made all the decisions beforehand for my boys and they were ok with it.

When I reported to the women's prison I was assigned to a solitary confmement room because feelings ran high within the prison for a person like me and they did it for my own security.

It was thirty days from hell! I did get to see my boys once a week but didn't want to see anyone else.

When I was released I went home, and the boys were allowed to return in time to start school. Joe was in St Rose of Lima and David was entered into a Head Start Program and we were on Public assistance with no income, I couldn't work because I couldn't drive. I started into a group therapy with Sylvia Weber MS,RN,CNS., which was in Providence and was picked up by one of the other "groupies" every week. It was time to start rebuilding my life and resolve the overwhelming depression I fmally acknowledged that was within me. The group was held in Providence on Benefit Street very near Brown University. In the group there were a variety of people, some medical, some trades, one PhD candidate from Brown, both men and women, all had issues they wanted to rectify. So I went, every week and tried to put my life in order, tried to understand the depression and the manner in which I had survived so far. I was not easy! Eventually I brought my love of poetry and how it had helped me in prison and finally understood that I had a responsibility to myself to help others.

I was on a good path at last with guidance of the group and its leader Sylvia Weber. I had brought some of the poems that I wrote in prison to the group and Sylvia introduced me to the new theory of Poetry as Therapy which was just getting started as a modality in psychiatric circles. Marlene Browne was very interested in my ability and love of poetry and felt that I should pursue a degree in the Classics at Brown. She told me that her mentor was Michael Harper, poet and professor at Brown. She introduced me to him on a day that I shall never forget. After I met him my life took on a new meaning, it had possibilities, Michael felt that I should open up my brain and write!!

Since I had to take the bus to wherever I would go, I found out that there was a bus to providence from the end of my street, so Brown was the only place I could go by myself. The next few months were filled with anxiety about how I was going to do it. At Brown they have a program for students who started a degree but never completed it, called the Resumed Undergraduate Education Program. I had credits from my first year at Salve Regina so I did qualify for the program. Now to be admitted to it was my next goal! I met with Mark Curran the dean of RUE for an interview. Michael Harper had recommended me on the merits of my writing so it was up to Mark Curran to assess my potential. I was so nervous! With my record and all my past I didn't know what to expect! I told him everything about myself and how I got to this place, he listened carefully and I only remember one statement; "I think it's about time someone gave you a break" "I will admit you as a non-matriculating student until the time when you will fulfill the criteria to be matriculated".

AND SO MY NEW LIFE BEGAN!!

In February of 1976! took one course and did well, then in September of 19771 took three courses and again did well so that by February of 1977! was admitted as a degree candidate. I had been able to apply for scholarships, student loans and grants. Now I must decide on a concentration. Since I had a background in Medicine and Psychiatry and a gift of Poetry then Poetry Therapy was the perfect fit. Poetry as therapy was a new concept in the 70's and a very new concept to the Professors at Brown University. I developed an Independent Concentration in "Poetry As A Therapeutic Process" and centered my studies in English and Psychology. In 1980 I graduated with honors in independent Concentration and went on to be hired at Rhode Island Hospital Psychiatric Unit as a Psychiatric Nurse/Poetry Therapist where I would complete the 450 hours of practice in group therapy which was the prerequisite for certification as a "Poetry Therapist".

I cannot even begin to write how Brown University and the wonderful brilliant caring professors changed my life and allowed me to speak my voice. It was done through guidance through literature, history, poetry, psychology and interactions with them and other students. All of the poetry I wrote while under the guidance of Michael Harper reflects this, the pain, the joy, the awakening of the spirit that made me who I am today.

The Mystery of Life

For Joe, Elaine, Morgan and Joey Christmas 2019

I stood at the top of the mountain
Looking down I saw the sea
How to get there surely was A mystery to me.

I could jump or fly, but it seemed
Too far for me, and then I saw
Your tiny boat stopping, looking up at me
And I flew down into your arms
Thank you for saving me!!

Love forever Your Mom

The Healing Song

Inspired by Blowin' in The Wind, by Bob Dylan

How many mountains can I climb
Until I fall into the sea,
How many wars will I live through
Until I know I'll be free,
The answer my friends is blowing
In the wind and be kissed by the sea.

Come with me and we shall see
The memories I hold close to my heart
I will tell you of warriors and medics
Who saved us all without hesitation
And let us continue to live a life
Alive and caring for others.

It all started with my dad and my mom
Who taught me well throughout my life
And I learned to stifle and strife
And heal those who cried for help.

Now I ask you to do the same
Help someone in my name
There is no mountain that's too tall
And you will never take a fall.

Walking

in Search of Possibilities

My boys were the foundation upon which I would rebuild my life. They were my strength, we became "three against the world" as we often said to each other. That became our mantra to survive. Memories of that time flood my brain still to this day.

King of the Mountain

I am at the top of the mountain,
arms extended. I reach to grab
the sky, but my grip does not hold, and
I fall into the star-stretched universe.

Once as a little girl, I played king
of the mountain. I never made it
to the top, there was always someone
bigger and stronger than I playing
at king, and bigger and stronger than
he who was king.

The sky captures me, and I float
into my own subconscious,
screened in a cage. I am lost
and cannot get out. I cry, but no
one hears me; no one can fmd me.

Poem for My Boys

Once, I had to hold up the
huge weight of rocks.
That I was small didn't matter
because the rocks were my sons.
I would be strong enough.

They started as pebbles,
each of his own mind,
rolled in the earth of life.
They grew into solid stones,
feet in dirt, and heart in sky. I have let them go.
Now they hold me up.

Thank you for just being!

You Made Me a Mom

For Joseph, on Mothers' Day 2010

A long time ago,
I married a man
I loved as no other,
the union made more perfect
when God gave us a son.
We held you and dreamed of
the life that we would have,
never realizing what lay ahead
and the changes we would see.
We lived on for a little while,
and joy was in our home,
then darkness fell so quietly
we never heard it moan.

Love is blind, that is right, for I refused to see
the chaos that slept with me destroyed my family.
I don't remember many things, and that is left unsaid,
crystal crumbled, broken glass, a life was left un-led.
I could not repair or fix, as I was sliced too thin;
no one had prepared me for this life I found me in!

"Daddy's sick," I said to you, but you already knew.
"Someday soon he will be gone. I don't know what to do."
Slowly did we mend the hurt. Neither of us knew
where it would take us down the road as our family grew.

We were three against the world, as brother joined our life,
our motto strong as we strove on,
surviving night to night.

"Mom," you said those magic words that brought me back
to life. "We'll be okay. I will take care of you."

The years passed on, your brother grew you taught him all
you knew.
I somehow learned to be a mom, holding on to you.

This day is not for me, but you, a son who made me so
spectacular a mom that never stops to grow.

Walking
in the Darkness

Years of the Siege

I turned my face from you to the wall
and screamed,
"Never come back."

The shells fell all around, destroying everything
I knew or loved.
The street erupted, spewing sin, hate, and loathing, catching my
clothes afire. Flames lick up my legs; no one could save me.
Tears fell from my eyes
in torrents;
charred fingers clawed the spent earth.

I stood in the sea,
sword hung at my side,
tip dipped in tepid tide.
No one knew me.
The muck I stood in oozed
through my toes.
Alone,
I pulled free and
stumbled onto drier land,
tired
and arrived.

Whose fight was it, anyway?
"Not mine," I said.
It was the good one, the
One That Should Be Fought!

Now I have come to this,
a galleon of fearless soul hunters
on my shore, Captain Ahab at the helm,
his will in futile opposition
to the great white whale.
A sorry master cannot heed the cries
of destiny. Bloody, scarred, and pierced,
I swim forever free.

The Cave

Suddenly I found myself
In a dark, dark place
With trees everywhere
Where am I
How did I get here
If you only knew...
Help me get out
It is dark
And I am afraid
Who cares...
Pull me out
Of this cave

I Saw Two Red Flowers Lying on a Bed of Black Rocks

Two red flowers
Black stones beneath
You sent to me
A memory
Touched my heart
As to remember
We are not free
Until we can see
The dark, dark water
Upon which they lie
Touch it to make more
Is it tears?
Is it death?
How deep is the water?
How large is the stone?
Life will go on
And someday see
You are the water
I am the stone
Who is the flower
Resting there?

<h1 align="center">*Home Alone*</h1>

A dark house sits silently and waits for
The grace of fingertips to brush rooms
With luminescence
Craving the companionship of a crowed
Room, I turn on all the lights now
In conversation with electricity—
Suddenly not weighted by shadows
That hang over idled furniture
And droop into unreserved corners.
The hum of artificiality distracts,
Imagining footsteps unpaused
And conversations played out
Through thin walls

I delay this performance of light
Willing the switches to flip seamlessly, on their own accord.

Joey Healey

Bering Dawn

I must go on, I must go on,
In this time of pain within the blackness In this time without
color.

Blackness, nothing
Just another pot.

And the graceful birds swing on
Invisible strings above the rolling waves.

And I must go on
Though every last muscle of this
Fragile human frame
Has lost its voice to the will,
To the plea for relief of any kind,
And like a baby left alone,
The voices die.

All voices have silenced under the
Steel wheels of this machine.
I am a part of the crew,
We are a part of the boat,
And She is a part of us.
This is an existence.

In the cold steel blueness
I see the forms of seabirds

One with the wind and sea
Those forces of Nature
The wind from the great open sky
The waves pushing me.

And my heart keeps beating
Let me hold it fast
Let me reach into the endless well overflowing
For it is all, it is all I have.
It is hope.

And the coming of the dawn is my Self outside of myself,
The realization of my dream.
And it is only Love which carries me on,
Love in the absence of doubt.

The dawn is coming
In this hourless night,
With the violent clashes of
Steel on steel
In the violence of this endless game
In a place with no name
We are here, bold enough.
We're not afraid to ride.

David Healey

Walking

with a Love

<h1 style="text-align:center">A Voice</h1>

I hear a sound singing
But I can't make out the words
I listen, listen, then I heard
The music all around me
Then I feel the sound
Pounding through my bones
Its says you are older now
But you have nothing to dread
I will care for you till
Both of us are dead.

You Asked Me

And I said I was reading poetry
And you asked "why"
And I said "because it makes me think!"
Of what you said, of feelings,
Of pain, of joy, of sorrow
Mostly I feel them again
With the writer of the poem
And cry with you because
I also feel your pain and want
To lead you with me
To a life of peace.

You Answered Me

I said "I need you"
Deeper than you know
I need you in my soul
I need your love
To keep me whole.

You are my strength
In times of stress
You will hold my heart
In any mess,

When you answered
"It's great to be needed"
My heart skipped a beat
And I silently pleaded,

Love me forever and I will see
The mystery of life
Unfold before me.

Joey

Color and balance
You float with a firefly's ease
Dashing light and color in hidden coves, bringing Steady glow
to unknown, lighting fires of curiosity That crackle ad grow,
Stretching towards heights within reach, you bring us To earth
with grounded feet

Streaking color across a blank canvas sky, you move With the
fluidity of a dancing paintbrush, sparking Meaning into motion
Uniting hues with each paint stroke
Every corner you infuse
Breathes a new life of color and wonder,
Deepening vibrance and electrifying life,
Words have more meaning and the world feels more Alive
In the safety of your canopy, in the circles of your Energy, the
air is crisper and more gentle,
Like breeze swept through a willow tree, you lift up Those
around you, and let them be, a certain freedom That's rare and
new, the strength and passion you Imbue, is inherent to your
soul and truth

Your love and inspiration falls in sheets like mid-may Rain,
washing away pain and kissing the earth so Flowers may bloom
and sway in the breeze of your

Beautiful ease,
A healing balm, a soulful song, the moon's glow at Night and
the sun's dazzling light, your existence is a Blessing, an un-
matched swirl of soothing bright and Soaring flights

Sofia

My Painter

For Joey

If everything else were sketched in pencil, erasable and thin,
He inks on tattooed bones,
A force of magnetism that draws me in
Colored pencils
Stained hands and hidden streaks of acrylic
On his body, a hidden for future discovery.
Sometimes I may point to them, but he feels
Their pull beyond optical strength

He fixes his gaze and it reminds me I'm
Alive, wanting to float in his iris and
See how he molds air and space into
Color and wonder

Languages of transferrable touch, intersecting
Like converging points of imaginative matter

Sofia

Mature Love

It's mature love I seek,
      distracted not am I
for house and home to keep.

It's mature love I seek,
      distracted not am I
for sensuous pleasures reap.

It's mature love I seek,
      distracted not am I
for loss of my demean to weep.

For life, like water,
      through fingers doth slip
seek I the simple pleasure
      of your companionship.

Griff Jones

Tonia

Can memory of passion be pressed
        like a rose in a bible
to be opened one day
        to answer a quibble?

What removes man's first passion
        as age turns him chaste?
Is there a golden realm for memory
        one wishes to forever encase?

The sounds of the past do land
        upon the present for to bind,
like gentle waves upon the sand,
        a murmur pleasant and kind.

Through her I found the world.
        It's still a mystery to me,
how a woman can introduce a man
        to his own deceit to see.

I came to her with the conceit
        that I was separate and apart.
She taught me it was just a belief
        held in the head, not in the heart.

To late! To late! Times takes it's flow,
        but can I tell of the memories she gave me?
But now! But now! Dare I tell her I finally know,
        her gift will in my sole always be.

Griff Jones

Walking
at the Water's Edge

I See

Steam rising off the ocean
Wind blowing my sails away
Snap that shutter I will say
So we can sail another day

For The Joy of Sea

On a beautiful sunny day, I walked down by the ocean
Then I plunged into the dark, dark sea
Hoping the ocean would let me be
I wanted to see the past sprayed before me
Crushed by the waves in the dark, dark sea.

But who would help me?
My mind went over and over the ones I love
But I could not see beneath the water
Or beneath the dark, dark sea
Help me, help me! I screamed aloud!

Then some ones body crashed into the
Ocean without a sound!
Im here to help you, come with me
I love you forever and you will see
The sky will open and you will be free.

The Fog is So Thick

I cannot see the ocean, boats pounding by
Birds flying in confusion cannot see
The tall trees standing on the edge
Of time where I am waiting
For the fog to melt away
Sending the sun for a better day.

Take a deep breath, Morgan said
You will have nothing to dread,
So I do, and follow you into the place
Of peace.

Waiting for the Sun

Blue sky, white puff
Pass me by
White snow crystals
Fallen on my hands.
There is the sun
I cant understand
Why it can't reach
My cold, cold hand.

Ever darkness
Ever dawn
Never learn
To lean upon.

Lost in mind
Cannot see
Door is closed
Near to me.

Beckon your Shattered glass
Shards of glitter
On the grass
Surround the sea Come to me.

Out Sailing on the Sun Kissed Sea

Out sailing on the sun kissed sea
A tiny voice whispered to me
Hi, it's Morgan, I'm ok
Getting through another day.
One lesson that I've learned well
Some men do come straight from hell
But many others that I love
Are sent to me from God above.
That thought inside warms my heart
Now I know where to start
To heal the past, express my fear
I talk to those that I hold dear.

Queen of the Ocean (Tonia)

Queen of the ocean,
Mother of the sea:
Your tides heal,
Your waves save.

An endless swell of joy and ease,
Your presence brings peace,
As an orange August sunset or a sailboat out to sea,
You wrap the ones you love in a cloak of salted breeze,
Guiding us home,
Fulfilling all needs.

By some lucky gust of wind
Or a shooting star whose wish was promised,
I found your grandson at the shore:
His heart is gold and intentions are pure,
A blessing real and true,
I like to think that you
Were behind this stroke of fate:
Steering the helm,
Coating the canvas with paint.

You place tidepools of inspiration in us all,
Bubbling saltwater wells roused by your wisdom and self,
Overflowing with admiration and creation:
We are the stars in your constellation,

Shining and winking to the rhythm of your innovation,
Gather around you, collecting heat and light,
Like a campfire's glow or a firefly at night.

You are the lighthouse's beacon in stormy weather;
The waves that carry the current that tethers:
A powerful force of material swirls,
You wash and take us as we are:
Held by the blue,
Safe in your arms.

Sofia

Moon Runes

By the light of the moon.
Several stones are strewn
Across these pages blank
And bare.

Forever I care, all the world
Is there and there
And destiny calls on rigid
Fearless forms of steel long
And tall, solid walls,
Constructions welded,
Destinies melded.
Of wayfaring souls of the sea.

'twas long ago, standing
With little hands, that
The awesome chord was struck.

A channel not wide,
A vessel inside,
Destined for Manissean's Isle.
And the seagulls in their cacophony,
Amidst a flood of air drenched with
Salty scent,
Floating, floating, floating.
Into the mystery.

The fog, the fog of the sea
Drifted into a silent realm,
Oh, inside, inside,
Words are naught to describe.

Shifted, transfixed I,
Bound in awe, by the
Immortal Croon of Neptune.

David Healey

Walking with a Friend

Dear Dr. Roye

Hands that heal
Hold the world.

Thank God for
Your hands
Thank God for
You.

We now have a life
To hold our hands
To God to thank
For God did heal.

Blessings in this New Year
Thankfully, Tonia Healey and Joyce Hickey

For Tenley I

You are the wind that fills his sails
You are the love of his heart
You are teller of his tales
Never to come apart.
So sail on my friend!

For Tenley II

The ocean is the joy of life
We watch it crest and flow
How it guides us without strife
We will never know.

But a sailor does realize
The time and motion of the tide
 The rocks and sand beneath her feet
Will show her where to meet
Anchored by the lines of love
And blessed by God above.
Continue onward my friend!

Greenland

For Tenley

I stood at the top of the mountain
Stretching my arms to embrace the air
My eyes filled with love
When I looked down at the ocean
Feeling the wind whip my sails
To bring me home to you.
I breathe deeply overcome
By the magnitude of it all.

We sail through the mountains of ice
See the sculptures that God has created
Watch them flip and melt, and I cry
For I know they will be gone in time.
Will they still be here when my boys
Return to follow the journey of their father?
I do not know but I will hold the memory
Of this time in my heart forever.

Finding Myself

As I struggled to find myself
I turned to poetry because as you said
"poetry has the potential to enhance
Our seeing, and even more importantly
Our ability to feel the poignancy and
Relevance of our own situations, our own Psyches, and our
own lives." (p. 27)

Poetry has helped me look inside myself
And see what is actually so.
I sit on the sand, the ocean surrounding
Me holding the stone, I find my soul.

(work of an unknown student)

The Yoga Master

For Deb

Reach toward your soul
Stretch your arms and touch
Your sprint, wait, wait then
Breathe deeply, clear your mind
Of thoughts inside, feel your heart,
The beating vibrates through your body
And then, open your eyes and look at me
Clasp your hands and say "Namaste"

The Root of My Soul

For Griff

Two tall trees standing on the edge of time
We insist that they speak to us
But they are silent in their magnificence
But wait, I hear a storm coming
Listen to the wind it has a story.

The wind will come, strong and fierce
Pouring through the forest, whipping us
Into dust, but we will not bend
We will fight, buried in the earth so tight,
Live to see another light.

Then I look up, so high, so high and I start to cry
Tears run down my face, I don't know why
I see the sun shining through the trees
I can't help but fall on my knees.
Bathed in warmth, surrounded by love
I see the mystery of who is above.

I will walk through the forest
In peace and love
With you beside me
And Him above.

Dig Deep

For MM

You harvest from the ocean
More than shells, but food
That feeds us in many ways
Brightening our dark days.

Water is your friend, the ocean
The pool, wherever you are
The water calls, you answer
To make it perfect again.
Thank you for your love of water.

The Traveler

For Loraine

You have traveled me far and wide
Guided me beyond my dreams
To places I could ride the tide
And sail safely back to my home

For these years of my life, since we started
So long ago, no in my aged mind
I remember my travels and relive them
My soul sings, my heart swells, and
I send my thanks to you.

Always, Tonia

Walking

with My Family

❧❧

Happy Birthday Grandma!

What can I say to Grandma on her birthday?
That will light her up, in this time of grey
She should firstly know, as I do internally
How very special she is to me
I don't take for granted, the care that she gives
Nor her endless love, and willingness to forgive
She's my ultimate role model, for she is so sage
I yearn to be just like her, when I turn that age!
I truly do admire her, for her life hasn't been easy
When I tell my kids her stories, I doubt they'll believe me!
That is precisely what I'll do, just as she did with me
Because in her lies my sole connection, to our history
Through her name I will maintain our family legacy
The Happiest of Birthdays to Grandma, the Big 80!

Love,
Joey

Ode to a Motorbike

I find peace on the back of a motorbike clutching on
Will carry me the right way
Squeezing thighs and a hum between my legs
I find peace in the nonexistent traffic lights
The flow of traffic
The gaps and spaces
Filled, soon with people and engines
Filled with creation and ablation.
I find peace in the wind on my face
In the forced solitude of holding on for dear life
In the billboards I pass by
I find peace in knowing that
No matter how far I roam
There is always a way home

Morgan

Wisdom

Since prehistoric times
humankind has sought
the reasons and rhymes
that bind us throughout
and keep the Big Wheel spinning
The Sages have a function
born in the Beginning
as integral people
to guide and protect
to warn and condone
they're the eyes of compassion
in the tribe and the home

What has been passed down
by word of mouth
has always saved us—
reinforced and deepened
our connection to Truth
In story and myth
in history and tradition
in sayings and values
the thread that knits
a people together

Wisdom, won through time and persistence
pain and perseverance
observation and reflection
failures and triumphs

endings and starts
all coalescing like tributaries
into a great river
an overflowing sum
surmounting its parts

It's deeper than Seascapes
more spacious than Space
Freer than free
Owing no one It's place
For It simply is
and It knows that It's great
It's the Sage's best friend
Powerful to create
Wisdom grew with us outward
from the ancient painted caves
now towards the spacecraft
on Red Planet plains
The balancing force
to our innate curiosity
Our unquenchable thirst
to reach our Destiny

Wisdom is the sextant
in our spiritual evolution
It fuels and carries
revolution after revolution
because only It can
Radiating Itself through
The crystal mind of the Sage
In the simple

yet intricate view
of lines She ties
from cause to effect
from this to that
from inquiry to explanation
from forest to skies

On Wisdom we are dependent
that's why the Gods bestowed It
into our mortal roles
It dwells inside our minds
and feeds into our souls
It bears light in the darkness
saving us the disgrace
of making the same old mistakes
Or of never extending
beyond a limited range
spanning from large to small
Social, emotional, rational, All

This great Power possessed
by those liv-ed long
whose stories all show
the wounds and the wrongs
transformed into what they know

Surviving life's trials
emerging battle-tempered, augmented
Warriors of the soul
not hiding in denial

Seeing
beyond a childlike shallow grasp
the holder of Wisdom
likens a profound
Giant Sequoia Tree
with its roots buried firmly in Earth
and its branch tips stretching
high in the sky
So magnificent is Her presence

Ones who have learned
their lessons inside
heeding reasons and rhymes
emerge in the fullness of time
Wisdom is theirs
Wisdom they give
These people who know
instruct us how to live

For Athena is Great and
Odin is All-Father
they are
Divine Wisdom
present in the Universe
Together they pervade
Its stellar tapestry
and inside you and me
defining the Origin of life
Thus the Sage knows that
Her Wisdom is consubstantial
with the One Wisdom

Through counsel with the Wise
Humanity shall continue to rise
To this the Gods testify
Mahatma Ghandi and Dr. King
taught the world
Many wise things
through their noble examples
Aggression is never the cure
to society's problems
Non-violent resistance
is the path to Peace
of this we can be sure

Wisdom emanates eternally
in the light of the Olympic flame
and the wreath of olive branches
protected by pure white doves
Wisdom speaks to us in our legacy
of poetry, literature and art
Wisdom is the foundation for
crucial decisions of great leaders
from every nation
and within every clan
Wisdom is always inclusive
and never seeks to destroy
but gathers unto itself
the varied dimensions of human existence
and sanctifies them, baptizes them
in purity, goodness and hope

Wisdom, sufficient unto Itself, from which nothing can
ever be taken away

is a storehouse of pure gold
is a river teeming with spawning salmon
is a perfectly baked loaf of bread
is a master Kindergarten teacher
is a brilliant star of hope
beckoning us
towards the Eastern mountain's slopes

Seek counsel in the Wise
It is your inheritance and ours
Share your thoughts and feelings
with ones who have built towers
To you they will listen and help
ascertain what lies hidden within
the penumbra of your ignorance
the hamartia of your sin
Inspiring you to dare ever further
overcoming fear and shadows black

Journeying inside and afar
there is no going back
Set your sights upon yonder star
Rise up to become fully who you are
build your eternal
Stronghold of Wisdom
Granite and marble
make It's polished floor
You were born to enlighten
With the golden key to It's door

For Mom from Davey
Happy Birthday 2019
April 27th Cambridge, MA

Happy Birthday to My Beloved Aunt Tonia

Whose love and fortitude has inspired me since I was a little girl into maturity.

The shelter of your heart in my childhood kept both me and my sister

Tara safe, despite the chaos surrounding us.

I am grateful beyond words for the times I have been honored to

Witness you demonstrate the power of one's truth and vulnerability.

Your example has taught me so much about the infallible strength of a

Woman when she is determined to carry on; pressing onward into the

Challenging work of healing beyond trauma.

You have always been a patient Mother of my Soul's journey through

Tragedy and triumph.

I love you eternally.... Christine

Homecoming

God is and always has been there. In the place I first looked. God is in the natural. God is in the bubbling stream, the sweet smell of flowers, the strength of the trees that I caress. God is in the touch on my leg that stroked me as I stood, naked, with water streaming across the crown of my head. God is in me. The light in me. God is the laugh when I watch my monkey mind, the narration. God is the warmth in my stomach, forgiveness, the release. Finding my body, this radiant being, back in the same place I began, with a smile. Of course it's you - it's always been you. Like coming back home to a crackling fire, palms open to feel the warmth. Like hugging my mom after a long day. Walking the same, ancient path with a fresh set of eyes. With a heart of joy, a laugh, and a smile. Standing naked, taking up space in this jungle, dirt between my feet, feeling the air of my exhale below my nose. I have come home.

This indescribable feeling, the release of the need to explain, the humor and laughter that comes with watching my mind try to do so anyway. This container, this heart full of so much love, so much light, such expansive space. There is no amount of straying or forgetting, no number of times where I wander and find myself lost, nothing that is too much to be forgiven, accepted, and brought back, right here. There is no limit to my love, this love, God's love. I rest in this space with a smile. Thank you for bringing me home.

Morgan Rose Healey

You Too, Sing America

You too, sing America
Yet you don't seem to see
Not everyone is happy, not everyone is free.
The carpenter, the mason, the shoemaker all sing,
Never truly looking, at what they're worshipping.

Sing America! Sing it blithe and strong!
But never will I sing it, 'til it be restrung.
The foundation is built on oppression,
Yet no one seems to put into question

Why sing America?

Land of the Free? Home of the brave!
More accurately - home to the ones who crave
Money, power, greed, fame.

Let us be the new United States,
And let us act and govern with love, not hate.
I assure you, we will then live in a democracy,
We will then live by the laws of liberty.

We too will sing America.
Joey Healey

Acknowledgements:
Inspired by Langston Hughes "I Too Sing America

Hi Morgan

I am grandma bear
Here to hold you
Have no fear
When you are sad
I'll be near,
If you are angry
You can hit me
Cause I can take it.
I'm strong you see.
When you are having fear
You can whisper in my ear
I'll hold your secrets
Oh so near.
And when you are happy
Hug me tight
Cause I love you
With all my might.

Love forever,
Grandma Tonia

My Dad

You teach me to discover
You help me to dream
You show me how to reach the sky
And places in-between.

I never have to turn around
To see you following behind.

I know wherever I go
Whatever I do
You are always there
Right next to me!

I love you daddy!!

Dear Joe, A Thanksgiving Note

I thank you every time
I get a pedi, mani or cut
see a good movie, or fill up my car,
go to the market or take a train
I thank you every time again.

When I sleep in my warm cozy bed
and wake in the morning with nothing to dread
I gaze out the window and see the sun
and thank you every time my son.

A long time ago when life was so hard
I didn't know if I could be, the mom
you needed to help you grow
and raise your brother all in tow.

So scarred was l, full of anger and pain
no place to turn to stop the rain.
until you said, "it's all right mom, we'll find a way
if we hold hands we'll be ok."

You stood and watched your father die
holding our hands we all did cry
a life so wasted he never knew
how his children rose and grew.

And so my son, on this day
I give thanks in every way,
for my sons so strong and bright
I never have a dreadful night.

I know you will continue to live
your life with so much more to give,
I am so proud of who you are
my life, my love, my shining star!!

Always, With Love, your Mom

Fifty Years of Love

For my Joe 07/31/16

I remember fifty years ago I held a tiny bundle of joy
You were peaceful and calm nestled in my arms,
And I knew from that moment that God had given
Me something very special that would change my life.

A child does wonderous things to you
It shapes you, moves you, challenges you
And takes your soul to new heights where
You find the peacefulness you seek.

Sometimes you don't know how to put
Food on his plate, clothes in his closet,
Books in his hand, but you do,
Cause you're a mom, he gave that gift to you.

When your brother came along, you took him
Under your wing and helped him grow into a strong
Young man, another gift for me.

And so my son, on this big day, I want to thank you
In every way for giving me purpose, drive and strength,
To be your guide these fifty years, and know
I will love you till the end of my day.

Happy birthday my son, I love you

My Dream

For Joe

I had a dream last night
I saw your face looking for me
Through the fog and rain
I try to reach out, but to no avail
Imprisoned in this dark, dark jail.

When will it end? I don't know
When is it safe to hug you close
When will I be able to hold your hand
I try, but really don't understand.

So my son, just take a ride
Through the darkness in my mind
Come rest your head by my side
And chase away this rough, rough tide.

Love from your Mom.

Thank you for sending him
To fix the water on the floor
Now I can really cleanse myself
And walk warmly out the door.

One never knows how dark it is
Unless you don't have a shower
But now I know, for I have been
Without that luxury for many an hour.

But you sent an angel to me,
Through the blinding snow and falling rain
He fixed the water and the floor
And I thank you forevermore.

Fire Island

For Elizabeth

My grandfather built me a room
hanging off the house, a limb of glass.
Even through the thickened panes, the waves
roared and tamed the sway of wild grass,
struck and blazing with 5:00 fire.
We hushed, only melted tangerine was left.

Hiding was easy among the grass,
pixies brushed my face with wings of glass
Beneath soaked deck boards, I made a room
of purple daydreams, caught on fire
burning, crackling, until the slanted rays left,
Welcoming sticky nightfall in humid waves

And the smell of steam and hot butter filled the room,
My mother danced around the stove in a dress made of sea
glass,
As grandma's hands cradled the fire,
And I reached only to their kneecaps, green with stained grass
As they salted and stirred in lulled waves
and the lobster boiled in the pot, his claw leaned left

Their faces glowed around the table in waves
of flickering light, the shadows left
and returned like cycles of conversing fire,
Her smile shone like glass,

stretching and pure. Balmy laughter soaked the room,
dew drops landing on tender grass.

And when the rain came down in tendrils of wet glass,
The spine of that little room
Shivered and bent, as if tossed by a wave
As I peeked through the meshed canopy of fire,
circling my bed of patched grass,
in rings of warmth. Despite the surge, the heat never left

Until memories were auctioned, fragile as thinned glass
Stolen light gasped, swallowed by darkened waves
And the eggshell room
Was cracked, shards packed up in stiff boxes of dried grass.
A pile of colorful ashes, remnants of the Fire
And given no choice, no soothe for bruises, we left.

You could always hear the steady whisper of the waves,
Even as we stared at the burnt island from the ferry, on fire.
And I think of the once-mine glass room, I know I've never
left.

Sophia

Walking

Towards an End

Finding Life

In honor of my 80th Birthday Party

I am a rock
I am an Island
A rock feels no pain
And an Island never cries.

Back in the day, as Simon said
"I have my books
And my poetry to protect me
I am shielded in my armor
Hiding in my room, safe within my womb
I touch no one and no one touches me,"
But all that changed so suddenly
I walked across the green at Brown University
To a class in Human Studies by Professor
George Morgan, and there my life was changed!

Professor Morgan taught us to look inside ourselves.
Morgan was engaged in "an intellectually rigorous
Critique of rationally" and I read his book and all
The others he gave us to study and I bloomed!

I broke the rock, it shattered into warm pebbles
I swam away from the Island to my new life
My profession and my boys.
They were with me all the way on this hard journey
Growing into the great men that they are now.

As I grew and grew older and wiser
I knew I had to find someone who loved me
And stay with me for the rest of my life.
Then I found the 'Joy of Sea'
The joy and the sea! What more could I need
Thank you- Joyce, I love you too!

Love Tonia

Waves Of Thought

They came rolling into my brain
I could not feel nor see the pain
The waves crashed over me
And here I was in the dark dark sea.

My brain is now gone, my memory also
But slowly I see that there is a link
Someone above who will help me
Rise above this sorrow before I sink
And lead me to tomorrow.

I searched and searched until
I felt your strength reaching out
To bring me back into my soul
And let me be whole again

And so read on my friend
And you will see my life and
How I came back with open
Arms to hold on to you.

The Mountain of Life

For Everyone I Love

I have climbed the mountain of life
It was a difficult climb at first
But now that I am at the top
I rest and recover with all of you
Now my life is taking on a new path
I am here to heal others and renew
My life time vows of loving each one
Of you until the day that I am gone
That is far away, but remember this
I love you and you helped me grow
Into who I am today, and so I say
Thank you, thank you all for this
Wonderful life!!!

Silence

Look, feel inside

Your soul is silent

Stop the clutter

Feel the quiet

Hold it until it warms you

And nothing there

Except silence

Thank you to:

David Okerlund

Joyce Hickey

Sofia Bagdade

Joe Healey

Joey Healey

David Healey

Morgan Healey

Christine Healey

Luther G. Jones III

Tara Picard

The introduction to this collection of poems and prose by and for Tonia offers an organization for the pieces included. The themes of light and dark, love and loneliness, and the fullness of life uplifted by family and friends forms the filter through which we experience the book. All of those themes are given unique and powerful expression as individual voices are blended into this collective work.

But what is the book about?

This is a book about healing. It is about the need for and possibilities of continual, deep, life changing healing. Tonia is a Poetry Therapist. This work is a part of her vocational calling and personal witness to the power of poetry to assist with our everlasting need to heal the mind and spirit.

Tonia Teresa Healey is a retired Psychiatric Nurse, living in Narragansett, Rhode Island. She is a certified Poetry Therapist of the National Association of Poetry Therapy. After becoming a nurse, she attended Brown University where she did an independent concentration, titled Poetry as a Therapeutic Process. She is also an "Army Brat" having grown up all over the world with her Dad.